# Social Media in the Professional World

## Professional World

*Networking and Beyond*

# Table of Contents

We don't have a choice on whether we do social media, the question is how well we do it.

--- Erik Qualman

# Chapter 1. Introduction

In an increasingly digital world, how you navigate social media platforms can drastically influence not just your social life, but your professional one as well. Our Special Report unveils the multidimensional realm of 'Social Media in the Professional World: Networking and Beyond.' Feel the enthusiasm as we delve into how different social media platforms shape professional spheres, how one can utilize these networks for career progression and even recruit talent. It isn't all dry and dusty information though; our report comes complete with fabulous infographics, real-life success stories, and expert tips to help you wield social media as a powerful tool in your career. When you're ready to power-up your professional world with a dash of digital dynamism, buy our Special Report. It's time to embrace the exciting possibilities that social media offers!

# Chapter 2. The Rise of Social Media in Professional circles

Social media, a term that was practically non-existent a couple of decades ago, has now permeated every sphere of our lives. It's incredibly diverse domain extends from maintaining personal relationships, to influencing global politics, to reshaping professional arenas. It is the latter that compels us to inspect it closely; the rise of social media in professional circles is a phenomenon that cannot be overlooked, but rather should be explored, understood, and ultimately, mastered.

## 2.1. The Dawn of Digital Networking

Before we revel in the present, a traipse down memory lane is in order. The dawn of the digital age in the late 1990s ushered in new tools and technologies that gradually evolved into the social media platforms we know today. Back then, it was rudimentary sites like Geocities and Blogger that allowed users to create their own websites or pages. These platforms let individuals experiment with an online persona, often extending their professional identity onto the digital world. LinkedIn, founded in 2002, took this a step further by positing itself as a network for professionals. Despite a slow start, it grew into the behemoth we know today, hosting approximately 740 million professionals. The ascent of LinkedIn marked a key shift in how career-oriented individuals networked and sought opportunities.

## 2.2. Modern Social Media Platforms and Their Influence

Fast forward to our immediate present and it's evident that social media has leapt far beyond LinkedIn. Major players like Twitter,

Facebook, Instagram, and many others have all carved a niche for themselves in the professional realm. Facebook pages promote businesses and services, Twitter serves as an instant podium for ideas and insights, and Instagram showcases creative portfolios and product displays. Even YouTube, a platform predominantly known for entertainment, has become a hub for educational content, product reviews, DIYs, and brand marketing, often acting as an indirect recruiting tool by hosting career advice and promotional videos concerning notable companies. Indeed, to borrow from Marshall McLuhan, the medium has become the message! These platforms influence not just direct business activities but also shape corporate cultures, user behavior, and professional trends.

# 2.3. Shifting Paradigms: From Formal Interactions to Empowered Relationships

A profound change that the rise of social media has brought forth is the transition from hierarchical, formal professional interactions to more democratic and empowered relationships. Social media provides an equal platform to all its participants, allowing everyone to voice their opinions, showcase their skills, and put their best foot forward across social strata. Interactions are no longer restricted by geographical boundaries or rigid office hierarchies; employees can interact with CEOs, customers can dialog with brand managers, and job seekers directly connect with potential recruiters. More importantly, these interactions are no longer one-off encounters, but rather, continuous conversations.

## 2.4. Networking Enhanced: Making Connections and Building Resilience

The professional field has capitalized greatly on social media as a robust networking tool. It allows professionals to connect with peers, mentors, industry leaders, and even potential employers from around the globe with just a click. The richness and diversity in the connections made online often surpass those made in traditional networking settings, like conferences or seminars. Additionally, they serve as a safety net during tough times. For instance, during the COVID-19 pandemic when conventional face-to-face networking opportunities ground to a halt, people turned to social media to maintain and even expand their professional connections, thereby demonstrating its resilience and indispensability.

## 2.5. Future Prospects: The Continued Rise of Social Media in the Professional Sphere

As we stand on the precipice of the future, the role of social media in our professional lives seems destined to broaden and deepen. Crowdsourcing ideas, remote collaboration, refined talent attraction, and uniquely personalized marketing are just some of the many avenues waiting to be further explored and utilized. Furthermore, the rise of new platforms such as TikTok and Clubhouse betoken the continuous evolution of this digital landscape.

In sum, social media has woven itself into the very fabric of professionalism, reshaping strategies, empowering individuals, strengthening connections, and propelling innovative approaches. The rise of social media in professional circles is no longer a novelty but rather a reality, whose full potential is yet to unfurl. As we journey alongside this digital revolution, anchorage in the knowledge of its past trials, present triumphs, and future possibilities is pivotal to sail successfully.

This chapter merely introduces you to the phenomenon that is the rise of social media in professional circles. The coming chapters will offer greater insights into understanding different platforms, creating compelling professional profiles, and leveraging these resources effectively. Let's march onward towards digital proficiency in our professional communications.

# Chapter 3. Understanding Different Social Media Platforms

Understanding the myriad social media platforms available today requires a comprehensive, nuanced approach. Each platform has distinct characteristics, from the type of content that populates its feeds, to the demographics of its user base, to its usefulness in a professional context. Many platforms can serve as powerful networking tools both online and offline, offering opportunities for professional growth and even, at times, innovative ways of working.

## 3.1. Facebook: Uniting the Personal and Professional

Facebook, that behemoth of social media platforms with over 2.8 billion monthly active users worldwide, was initially conceptualized as a way for Harvard students to connect. Since then, it has evolved into a platform where personal connections abound, but professional ones can thrive as well.

Facebook Pages allow businesses and brands to curate an online presence, sharing company updates, job postings, and relevant industry content. Facebook Groups serve as communal spaces for individuals with similar interests, including professional ones, to interact, share ideas, and seek advice. Plus, with the launch of Facebook Jobs, users can also seek employment opportunities directly on the platform.

However, the line between personal and professional on Facebook can quickly blur, necessitating careful consideration of one's privacy settings and content shared.

## 3.2. LinkedIn: The Premier Professional Platform

Often described as the professional's social media, LinkedIn reigns supreme when it comes to career development. The platform hosts over 760 million professionals, offering countless opportunities to build networks, gain industry insights, and showcase one's skills and experience.

LinkedIn provides a stage for creating an online resume via its user profiles – detailing experiences, skills, and endorsements from colleagues. Connections can be made with colleagues, seniors in your field, or even potential recruiters, aiding in networking efforts and possible job opportunities. The platform also sparks engagement through shared articles, blog posts, and even features like LinkedIn Learning and LinkedIn Jobs.

Given its definitive professional focus, LinkedIn demands a more sober, strategic form of communication compared to other platforms.

## 3.3. Twitter: Harnessing the Power of Brevity

Twitter's unique selling proposition lies in its speed and succinctness. Despite a 280 character limit, the platform hosts robust conversations, diverse opinions, and a constant inflow of news and updates.

From a professional standpoint, Twitter excels as an information source, allowing you to follow industry leaders, companies, and key influencers for real-time updates and insights. It also serves as an influential platform for establishing thought leadership, as the act of curating, sharing, and sparking conversations around relevant industry trends can help professionals position themselves as experts in their field.

But with great visibility comes great responsibility; Twitter's instantaneous nature demands careful thought and attention to ensure that content shared doesn't misrepresent oneself professionally.

# 3.4. Instagram and Pinterest: Showcasing Careers Visually

Instagram and Pinterest, both majorly image-driven platforms, have emerged as potent tools for certain industries to showcase work visually. Their focus on visual storytelling has made them particularly popular among creative professionals – photographers, designers, artists, and fashion professionals, to name a few.

Instagram's features like Stories, IGTV, and Reels allow for creative latitude, providing opportunities for professionals to take their audience behind-the-scenes, showcase their work process, and interact with them in a more candid, intimate manner.

Pinterest, on the other hand, serves as a digital mood board, enabling users to gather references, draw inspiration, and showcase their portfolios. Its unique structure encourages discovery, making it an interesting tool for professionals to gain visibility and demonstrate their aesthetic or vision.

# 3.5. YouTube: Leveraging Video for Professional Growth

YouTube, as the world's largest video-sharing platform, offers a goldmine of opportunities for professionals, particularly those in fields such as digital marketing, video production, and education.

From tutorials and webinars, to product demonstrations and reviews, to vlogs documenting professional journeys, the types of content that can be created and shared on YouTube are varied. The platform also serves as a learning resource, offering professionals the chance to upskill through countless educational videos and courses.

However, maintaining a professional YouTube channel requires significant dedication, and often, the skills to create and edit videos, demanding a larger time investment than other platforms.

In conclusion, navigating different social media platforms requires an understanding of each platform's individual strengths and weaknesses, the demographic it engages, and the types of content it best showcases. Leveraging this understanding can empower professionals to manage their social media use more strategically, and ensure they derive maximum professional benefit from their online presence.

# Chapter 4. Social Media Etiquette: Do's and Don'ts

In a society driven increasingly by digital forms of communication and interactions, understanding the etiquette of social media has never been more critical. This chapter will delve into the nuances of online behavior, listing the do's and don'ts that can dramatically influence your professional reputation on social media platforms.

## 4.1. Understanding the Importance of Etiquettes in a Digital Environment

In many regards, the etiquette expected on social media mirrors that of real-world interactions. However, the digital space introduces unique dynamics that professionals must consider. Online, your communication lacks the context that body language, voice tonality, and immediate responses provide in person. Consequently, your words and posts can sometimes be taken out of context, misconstrued, or scrutinized closely.

## 4.2. The Do's of Professional Social Media Etiquette

Let's start with the "do's," often overlooked and underappreciated, they form the core of a respectable online presence.

**DO curate carefully**: Good manners begin with attention to what you communicate. This includes posts, comments, shares, and even likes. Err on the side of caution, aiming for content that informs, inspires, or edifies.

**DO master the art of online listening**: Part of mastering social media etiquette involves observing and understanding the tone, content and context of an ongoing conversation before jumping right into it. Pay attention to what others say, and respond with thoughtfulness.

**DO engage, don't broadcast**: Social media is a two-way street. Instead of just broadcasting information or opinions, make sure to engage with others. Interaction fosters relationships and respect. Respond to comments on your posts and actively comment on others' posts as well.

**DO keep it professional**: Be mindful that your conduct can be seen by current or potential clients, employers, or colleagues. Refrain from posting inappropriate content or engaging in internet arguments. Maintain diplomacy, respect, and cordiality even during online disagreements.

# 4.3. The Don'ts of Professional Social Media Etiquette

Just as crucial as the positive practices to uphold, understanding and avoiding the pitfalls in social media etiquette can save your professional reputation from irreparable damage.

**DON'T over-share**: There is a fine line between being personable and revealing too much. The internet doesn't forget, so be selective with what you share, especially concerning personal information or sensitive matters.

**DON'T ignore others**: If someone engages with your content, be courteous and respond appropriately. Ignoring comments, messages, or feedback can portray you as unresponsive or disinterested.

**DON'T spam**: Bombarding your network with too many posts or irrelevant content can appear as spam, and deter people from wanting to interact with you. Quality over quantity is key.

**DON'T get too personal**: Even though social media channels are public platforms, it's essential to remember that not all topics are suitable for discussion. Divisive or sensitive topics such as politics and religion are often better left untouched.

# 4.4. In conclusion

In essence, mastering the etiquette of social media revolves around respect and consideration for others. Make it your mission to enhance the digital ecosystem, by sharing valuable content, engaging respectfully with others, and steering clear of practices that can leech the environment of its professionalism.

Bearing these web-wise do's and don'ts in mind will elevate your social media presence, safeguard your professional reputation and enable you to leverage the advantages that these platforms afford for networking and career growth. Always remember, online or offline, manners do matter. Develop and nurture your online reputation as carefully as you would your real-world one. In an era where so much of life is lived and experienced online, your digital footprint is nothing less than your newest curriculum vitae.

# Chapter 5. Building Your Professional Social Media Profile

Establishing oneself prominently on a social media platform should be a calculated endeavor, carefully designed and executed to project the right image. The following sections will guide you through crafting a social media persona that resonates with professional excellence.

## 5.1. Choosing the Right Platforms

First and foremost, determine the social media platforms you should be active on. These platforms should correspond with your professional objectives. If you are a creative professional looking to display visual content, then Instagram or Pinterest might be the most appropriate platform. For corporate professionals aiming to connect with recruiters and industry professionals, LinkedIn may be the most beneficial. Those operating in the media and communications or tech industries might find Twitter an invaluable platform, given its fast-paced information sharing. Be mindful of each platform's audience and use it to your advantage.

## 5.2. Creating a Consistent Brand Image

In the digital market, consistency is key. From your profile picture to your posts' tone, ensure that your social media profiles across all platforms have a unifying theme. This lends credibility to your claim of being a professional in a given field. A consistent use of colors, fonts, language, and tone helps in establishing your 'brand,' making you recognizable across the spectrum of social media channels.

## 5.3. Optimizing Your Bio

Once your platforms are chosen and a unified brand image is decided upon, turn your attention to your profile's headline or bio. This is often the first thing viewers engage with. Your bio should be concise, yet richly informative, offering a snapshot of who you are professionally. Include your current role, your areas of expertise, key achievements, and ways to connect. Keywords are crucial here, as they enhance discoverability in platform or Google searches. Use terms related to your profession, industry, and skills.

## 5.4. Tailoring Your Posts

The content of your posts is where you demonstrate your expertise and experience. However, beyond merely sharing information about your work, you should discuss industry trends, share relevant news articles, ask thought-provoking questions, and engage with your audience's content. This positions you as an active, informed player in your industry.

## 5.5. Interacting With Your Network

Merely creating and posting content isn't enough. Audience engagement is a critical aspect of social media management. Respond promptly to comments and messages. Start conversations. Share and comment on others' posts. Building a network is not only about growing the number of your followers or connections; it's about establishing relationships.

## 5.6. Using Visuals Effectively

A picture speaks a thousand words, and on social media platforms, effective visuals can boost engagement significantly. Whether it's infographics on LinkedIn, image quotes on Twitter, or photographs on Instagram, ensure your visuals align with your brand image and message.

## 5.7. Scheduling Regular Activity

Consistent activity keeps your profile in the feeds of your followers. By scheduling posts, responses, and shares, you maintain a regular digital presence, while still allowing yourself to disconnect and focus on other tasks. Tools like Buffer or Hootsuite can help manage your posting schedule.

## 5.8. Navigating Professional and Personal Content

While infusing your social media profiles with a personal touch can make them more relatable, maintain a distinction between professional and personal content. Revealing some personal interests or activities can help you connect with others on a deeper level, but ensure these posts still align with the professional image you want to present.

## 5.9. Reviewing, Reflecting, and Revising

Periodically, take a step back to review and reflect on your social media strategy. Consider what's working and what isn't. Analyze your post performance or use social media audit tools to gain insights. Based on these reflections, revise your strategy and update your profiles to present the most effective version of your professional identity.

In the ever-changing digital landscape, shaping and maintaining a professional social media presence requires patience, creativity, and strategic thinking. By following these tips, you'll cultivate a powerful online persona, opening doors to networking, learning, and career opportunities. The key is to stay engaged, stay consistent, and always be ready to adapt to the ever-evolving trends in social media.

# Chapter 6. Leveraging LinkedIn for Career Growth

Amid a plethora of social media platforms, LinkedIn emerges as a standout; an arena specially tailored for professionals across the globe. More than a decade since its inception, LinkedIn has transformed the way professionals connect, interact, and grow, securing its focal position in the online professional landscape. To truly harness the power of this remarkable platform, it's crucial to delve deeper into its variety of features, examining how to effectively leverage LinkedIn for a robust professional ascent.

## 6.1. Understanding the Framework of LinkedIn

LinkedIn, at its core, is a professional networking site, acting as a digital extension of your in-person professional activities. Your LinkedIn profile serves as your online resume, showcasing your skills, experiences, and career aspirations to potential employers, colleagues, or clients. The richness of this platform lies not only in its ability to host your professional snapshot but also in how it fosters connections, facilitates knowledge sharing, and opens opportunities for collaborations.

## 6.2. Setting Up Your Profile Correctly

The first step towards leveraging LinkedIn effectively is to an articulate and comprehensive profile. Pay attention to the details, including uploading a professional profile photo and crafting a succinct, engaging headline. The headline (right beneath your name) should reflect your current role, area of expertise, or career ambitions in less than 120 characters.

Completing the 'About' section is equally important, offering a window into your professional journey and goals. Aim to strike a balance between being professional and personable, allowing viewers to grasp your passion and dedication in your field. Dot-point or use paragraph-style writing to provide a content-rich summary, including your key achievements, skills, and career aspirations.

Apart from these, filling out sections like 'Experience,' 'Education,' 'Licenses & Certifications,' and 'Skills & Endorsements' can paint a robust picture of your professional trajectory. Your LinkedIn profile is also a powerful platform to showcase your work samples by linking blogs, articles, presentations, or video demonstrations in the 'Featured' section.

# 6.3. Maximizing Visibility with the Right Connections

Once your profile is set, it's time to make strong connections. LinkedIn encourages you to connect with people you know or with whom you've had a professional relationship. Mutual connections, shared professional interests, and being part of the same organizations or groups can facilitate the process of expanding your LinkedIn network.

Reach out with personalized connection requests explaining how you know the person or expressing interest in their work. Remember, quality over quantity is a crucial rule to follow when establishing connections. A handful of meaningful connections with professionals aligned with your interests and goals can be much more valuable than hundreds of random connections.

## 6.4. Engaging with Content and Staying Active

Constant engagement with platform content is key to staying visible on LinkedIn. Make it a habit to share industry-related posts, comment on updates from your connections, or engage in professional discussions. You don't have to produce original content every time; curating and sharing relevant content also counts. A compelling post or share can spark meaningful conversations, enhancing your professional reputation and visibility.

## 6.5. Leveraging LinkedIn for Job Opportunities

LinkedIn has rapidly evolved into a vibrant job market. The 'Jobs' tab lets you browse through hundreds of job postings tailored to your profile and preferences. Regularly updating your career interests and actively applying through the platform increases your chances of landing interviews.

Moreover, LinkedIn is not only about waiting for job posts; in this proactive platform, reaching out to recruiters, HR professionals, or employees working in your target companies could give you a competitive edge. A well-crafted message detailing your interest in the company and its work could lead to fruitful professional dialogues.

## 6.6. Using LinkedIn Learning for Skill Development

LinkedIn Learning, the platform's educational arm, offers a wide array of courses across industries and fields. Availing of these can prove a testimonial to your dedication towards continuous learning and skill enhancement.

## 6.7. Honing Your Personal Brand

LinkedIn is also a podium for personal branding. By regularly sharing industry insights, participating in discussions, and showcasing your work, you brand yourself as a thought leader in your field - an invaluable trait in today's competitive professional environment.

## 6.8. Coming to Grips with LinkedIn Etiquette

In your quest for networking and visibility, ensure you adhere to the unspoken professional etiquette on LinkedIn. Always keep interactions professional and polite and show appreciation when someone endorses your skills or writes a recommendation.

Understanding and adeptly leveraging LinkedIn can pave your career path to new horizons. With a meticulously crafted profile, meaningful networking, active engagement, and a commitment to lifelong learning, you're well-equipped to ride on LinkedIn's wave of opportunities towards career growth.

# Chapter 7. Twitter: Brevity and Impact in the World of Professionals

As humanity surges forward into an increasingly digital era, our traditional modes of communication are being reshaped, and new forms of interaction have emerged that are profoundly affecting both our personal and professional lives. One profound change comes in the form of the social media platform, Twitter. Although originally viewed as a social tool for sharing fleeting thoughts and updates, Twitter has evolved into a powerful channel for professional communication and career growth. In an environment where brevity is rewarded and substantial messages are often contained within just 280 characters, learning to harness the power of Twitter for professional use can have an immeasurable impact.

## 7.1. The Importance of Brevity on Twitter

Twitter's defining feature is its strict character limit in each tweet. Initially, this was just 140 characters, a limit which was doubled in late 2017 to its current 280. This encouraging brevity means professionals have to carefully select the language they use, as every character bears weight. These confines have sparked creativity, with users finding ingenious ways to distil complex ideas and narratives into succinct, bite-sized pieces of content. For those wishing to convey professional expertise or project a specific brand identity, mastering the art of brevity becomes paramount to achieving impact.

## 7.2. Building a Professional Image

As with any social media platform, Twitter allows users to curate their peer-facing image. What differs here, however, is the speed and frequency with which users can post, react to trends and engage in conversations. This provides a wealth of opportunities for professionals looking to reinforce their image or brand. However, with this opportunity comes potential pitfalls. Anything posted on Twitter becomes part of your online presence and could be accessed by potential employers, colleagues or industry peers. Maintaining a balance between authenticity and professionalism is crucial.

## 7.3. Network Building and Engagement

One of the key benefits Twitter offers professionals is the chance to build a network that extends beyond their immediate circle. Through following, being followed by and engaging with like-minded individuals, professionals can cultivate a rich network of influential contacts. The platform also allows for the disintegration of traditional hierarchical boundaries, giving users the potential to engage with professionals, experts and thought-leaders they may not have had access to otherwise.

However, caution must be exercised as engaging on Twitter also means exposing oneself to public scrutiny. Professional conduct on Twitter is, therefore, as important as in any other professional arena.

## 7.4. Leveraging Hashtags for Visibility

Hashtags, invented by Twitter, are a gateway to visibility on the platform. By using relevant and popular hashtags, professionals can increase their visibility and discoverability within their field. Hashtags also offer a way to join professional discussions and engage with recent trends, demonstrating to others your investment and understanding of your field.

## 7.5. Twitter as a Learning Resource

Twitter offers a stream of information, news, ideas and conversations that can prove invaluable for professionals who want to stay ahead in their fields. By following relevant accounts, subscribing to lists and disciplining their Twitter stream, professionals can make Twitter into an ongoing seminar in their pocket. Moreover, Twitter chats—designated conversations facilitated by pre-arranged topics and specific hashtags—offer rich opportunities for learning and networking.

## 7.6. The Double-Edged Sword of Twitter's Speed

Twitter's high-flow speed can be a blessing and a curse. On one hand, the rapid update of content ensures there's always something happening, a trend to join, and an ongoing conversation to become part of. However, the rapidity of Twitter can also lead to issues with fake news as well as content becoming obsolete quickly. Professionals must, therefore, discern what is worth their attention and what is not.

Navigating through the world of Twitter is not merely about survival, but learning how to thrive. Professionals should remember that while tool mastery is significant, it won't replace traditional values of honesty, integrity, and respect in the professional discourse. When properly harnessed, Twitter can become an outstanding tool in your professional arsenal. The professional journey on Twitter may be a marathon, not a sprint, but the rewards of connections made, knowledge gained, and impact created can be invaluable.

# Chapter 8. Instagram and Pinterest: Leveraging Visual Media for Work

In the current era of the digital revolution, where words are often overshadowed by graphics, Instagram and Pinterest are rising stars in the world of social media, particularly for professionals from creative domains. They offer a visually dominated platform to showcase creativity, generate influence, network with like-minded individuals and organizations, and ultimately chart new paths in career progression. Let's delve into the intriguing jigsaw of maneuvering these platforms to carve an enticing professional presence.

## 8.1. Embrace the Power of Visual Storytelling

Visual storytelling is a potent tool, marrying the art of narrative with compelling imagery to forge emotional connections. On platforms like Instagram and Pinterest, pictures–and by extension, visual stories–speak louder than words. They can depict your professional journey, projects, office culture, or even demonstrate your products or services, giving followers glimpses into your professional universe.

Create engaging content that goes beyond mere promotion. You might consider sharing behind-the-scenes glimpses of your work, client testimonials, or contextual narratives around your product/service. It's always valuable to weave a tale that elicits an emotional response, fostering a deeper connection with your audience.

## 8.2. Grasp the Essence of Instagram for Professionals: Profiles and Posts

Instagram is more than just a place for selfie lovers. It's a platform ripe for personal branding, networking, and most importantly, showcasing your work spectrum. A well-curated Instagram profile can serve as a visual resume that tells a compelling story about your professional exemplarity.

Optimize your Instagram profile for maximum visibility. Use a recognizable photo or logo, a username closely aligned with your real name or company name, and a succinct yet comprehensive bio. Don't shy away from adding contact information, necessary URLs, or buzzwords associated with your profession. Remember, your profile is your calling card.

On Instagram, content is queen. Regularly posting high-quality, engaging images or short videos related to your profession can elevate your standing in your industry. Make use of Instagram stories, reels, and IGTV to diversify your content, engage with your audience, and thus build a stronger professional network.

## 8.3. Dig Deeper Into Pinterest: Boards and Pins

In contrast to Instagram, Pinterest operates more like a search engine for images. It's a platform that businesses and professionals use to promote their brands, expand their reach, and attract traffic to their websites or blogs.

Create Pinterest boards around various facets of your profession or industry. Each board should have a distinct theme and a clear, descriptive title that incorporates keywords related to your field. Populate these boards with pins that are visually appealing and provide value to your potential audience. Remember to add detailed descriptions and relevant hashtags to each pin to maximize its discoverability.

## 8.4. The Art of Hashtagging and SEO in Visual Social Media

Hashtags can be a strategic tool for boosting your content exposure. They can help categorize your content, make it discoverable to a wider audience, and align your brand with trends or niches. But use them wisely. Stick to relevance over copiousness. Strategic use of trending and industry-specific hashtags can amplify your visibility in vast, digital crowds.

SEO isn't just for written content. Optimizing your content for search is essential on visual platforms too. Leverage keywords in descriptions, alt text for images, and even file names for maximum discoverability.

## 8.5. Analyzing Performance and Engaging with Your Audience

All your efforts should be backed by diligent tracking of performance metrics. Instagram Insights and Pinterest Analytics provide valuable data regarding post performance, audience demographics and engagement trends. Use these insights to refine your content strategy, post timings, and engagement techniques.

Interaction with your audience goes a long way in building credibility and rapport. Respond to comments, engage in conversations, and show gratitude for shares and mentions. This fosters a sense of community, ultimately nurturing professional alliances and collaborations.

# 8.6. Maintaining Professional Decorum and Ethics in Visual Media

While these platforms provide vast scopes for creative liberty, maintaining professional decorum and ethics is crucial. This includes giving credit where it's due, respecting copyrights, refraining from inappropriate content, and staying true to your professional persona.

In conclusion, Instagram and Pinterest offer professionals a unique outlet to display their work and talent in a visually impressive manner. By learning to harness their tools effectively, you can convert these platforms into ladders for career growth and networking. To be truly successful in the digital age, professionals must learn to embrace and utilize visual media platforms as they navigate their career paths.

# Chapter 9. Recruiting in the Social Media Age: How to find the Right Talent Online

The advent of social media has dramatically shifted the modus operandi of the recruitment landscape. How recruiters search for prospective candidates, interact with them, and evaluate their suitability for a particular role has been significantly transformed, with the digital sphere becoming a hotbed of talent and potential.

## 9.1. The Evolution of Recruitment

Before we delve into the tactics and strategies of recruiting in the social media age, it might be beneficial to establish the extent to which social media has fostered changes in the recruitment process. Prior to this digital revolution, headhunters mainly relied on print advertisements, job boards, or third-party recruitment agencies to locate and engage potential candidates.

Moving from these traditional methods to online job boards was the first significant revolution in recruitment. The second – and potentially more impactful – shift has been the widespread use of social media for talent acquisition. A survey from the Society for Human Resource Management indicated that 84% of organizations use social media for recruitment, highlighting the immense significance of this platform.

## 9.2. The Power of Social Media in Talent Acquisition

Social media is not just another platform for posting job vacancies.

Instead, it offers a multi-dimensional utility for organizations searching for new talent. Primarily, it serves as a tool to create a compelling brand image and disseminate it among potential candidates. Companies are increasingly leveraging their social media profiles to portray their culture, values, and work environment to attract like-minded candidates, consequently improving the quality of applications.

Additionally, social media allows hiring teams to proactively search for potential candidates, even if these individuals are not actively looking for a job. Sites like LinkedIn facilitate keyword searches for specific skills, educational qualifications, or previous job titles, helping organizations identify suitable profiles with ease. Furthermore, social media makes it possible for HR professionals to engage with these candidates directly and build relationships over time - a nuanced approach that enhances the overall recruitment strategy.

# 9.3. Strategic Use of Different Social Media Platforms

While LinkedIn remains the most popular social media website for talent acquisition, organizations can take advantage of various platforms to locate different types of candidates:

- LinkedIn: The premier professional networking platform, LinkedIn, is an excellent place to engage with individuals from every professional background. By using its advanced search functions and Group features, HR professionals can locate individuals who match the skills and experience required for a specific role.

- Twitter: A rapidly moving platform, perfect for locating influencers within a particular field. Recruiters can engage with potential candidates and follow hashtags associated with their industry to find talented individuals who might be latent job seekers.

- Facebook: Despite its reputation as a platform for personal connections, Facebook offers extensive potential for recruitment. Companies can utilize Facebook's job posting feature and search functions to find individuals with specific interests aligning with a job's requirements.

- Instagram: A visual platform that lets companies showcase their culture, work environment, and mission to prospective candidates who prefer a more interactive and visually engaging experience.

# 9.4. Navigating the Potential Pitfalls

While social media opens up numerous possibilities for recruiters, it also comes with potential pitfalls. Working in a digital environment means navigating the delicate balance between professional and personal boundaries. For example, evaluating a candidate's professional suitability based on their personal social media content can potentially lead to biased decisions.

Furthermore, the vast amount of data available on social media might lead to information overload, making it challenging for recruiters to identify truly promising candidates. Using data analytics tools, recruiters can sift through voluminous data and identify patterns that may assist in making more informed decisions.

Finally, recruiters must diligently respect privacy settings and norms associated with each platform. Overly aggressive tactics could be off-putting to potential candidates and damage the company's reputation.

# 9.5. Conclusion

Harnessing the power of social media for recruitment demands strategic planning and careful execution. It requires recruiters to actively engage with potential candidates, offer a realistic depiction of their company's culture and values, and respect digital etique. By doing so, they can leverage these platforms to locate the right talent, forging meaningful connections, and driving their organizations toward a more fruitful future.

# Chapter 10. The Storytelling Approach: Content Creation and Curation

The ability to weave engaging narratives can revolutionize the manner by which you connect with people. As such, storytelling has emerged as a powerful tool in professional social media usage, significantly influencing content creation and curation. Mastering this approach can lend a novel dimension to your digital presence, enriching your professional outreach and engagement.

## 10.1. The Art of Storytelling

Storytelling isn't merely the act of compiling a few events together and presenting them. At its core, it is a powerful artform that can change perceptions and move individuals to action like no other tool. Effective storytelling involves crafting narratives that draw audiences in, stir their emotions, and resonate with their experiences and aspirations.

The power of storytelling on social media lies in its ability to forge connections. It helps to humanize your persona or your brand, creating a stronger bond with your audience. Additionally, as per the 'Storytelling Potential', a concept propounded by Christian Salmon, stories tend to stick better than plain facts or features. Thus, incorporating storytelling into your social media strategy can cultivate an engaging professional brand image. It can turn you into a thought leader within your chosen field, and instill trust, fostering long-lasting relationships with audiences across platforms.

## 10.2. Crafting Captivating Narratives: Content Creation

Creating engaging content that tells a story can be challenging, yet profoundly rewarding. The trick lies in balancing between your professional objectives and the narratives that your audience can connect with.

Firstly, it's important to identify your brand's core values or your professional principles and weave a story around them. Always keep in your mind who your target audience is. Understand what they appreciate, what drives them, and how your narrative can resonate.

Secondly, always strive for authenticity. Authentic narrations are relatable; they underscore your values, re-emphasize your mission, and foster trust. Remember, stories are shared experiences; the more genuine they are, the more they resonate with the audience.

Finally, engage your audience. Don't just tell your story, have your audience live it. Use multimedia, like images, videos, or infographics, to make your narrative more immersive. Use interactive content such as polls or quizzes to keep the audience's attention and invite their participation.

## 10.3. Curating and Sharing Relevant Content

Content curation involves sourcing, organizing, and sharing information pertinent to your professional niche or industry. To put it simply, it is sharing third-party content with your audience on your social networks.

A simple way to maintain a productive social media feed is to share existing content that aligns with your professional principles, mission, and the interests of your audience. It is, however, not enough to just share any content; it must add value to your audience.

Bear in mind that curating content is not a substitute for creating your own. It should complement your original content, providing your audience varied perspectives and valuable insights from the wider industry.

# 10.4. The Power of Consistency

The power of storytelling extends not only in crafting individual narratives but also in maintaining a consistent narrative across your social media platforms. A consistent brand story across your social media profiles can help reinforce your professional message and strengthen your digital persona.

The art of storytelling in social media is indeed a game-changer. It has the unparalleled power to captivate audiences, provoke thought, and engender loyalty. Thereby, when employed tactfully, it is capable of opening avenues to connect and engage with peers, clients, or employers on a more profound level. Understanding and employing the principles of content creation and curation, and embedding narrative elements within them, can result in enhancing your professional image, and potentially expanding your career opportunities.

Immerse, hence, into the significant yet exciting realm of professional storytelling on social media. Remember, every interaction you have is a chance to tell a story, and every story you tell brings you one step closer to your professional aspirations. So, don't just share information, tell a story and make a lasting impact!

# Chapter 11. Securing your Online Presence: Safeguarding Privacy in Professional Social Media Use

In this highly digital age where virtually every professional is poised behind an online avatar, the security of your online presence is paramount. It is a challenging task as every day we are bombarded with unsettling news about security breaches, data mismanagement and privacy violations. This chapter aims to demystify online security and privacy issues surrounding professional social media use, and provide exhaustive tips, suggestions, and strategies for creating and maintaining a secure online presence.

## 11.1. The Importance of Privacy and Security in Professional Social Media Use

The world of social media is a bustling platform of interconnectivity, information sharing, and professional networking. However, it can also be a conduit of opportunities for cyber criminals, hackers, and data miners. These potential threats underscore the significance of maintaining privacy and security in professional social media use. Each careless click, each piece of data shared, can potentially expose archived web history, personal information, contact details, buying behavior and many more layers of privacy that all users should zealously guard.

## 11.2. Understanding the Landscape of Online Threats

To fully appreciate the need for online security, it's important to understand the landscape of online threats and the potential impact they could have on you as a professional. Cyber threats can take many forms, from phishing scams designed to steal your personal details, to sophisticated hacking attempts exploiting weak security systems. As we become more intertwined and dependent on our digital environments, these threats are escalating both in complexity and hazard.

## 11.3. Phishing Attacks and Social Engineering

Phishing and social engineering are common threat vectors that prey on human vulnerabilities rather than on system weaknesses. These methods trick individuals into divulging sensitive data like passwords or credit card numbers by pretending to be a trustworthy entity. In a professional setting, the stakes are even higher as it may involve confidential company data and resources.

## 11.4. Implementing Robust Password Practices

One of the simplest and most effective measures you can take to secure your online presence is to follow best practice with regards to password creation and management. Employing multifactor authentication, using unique passwords for each social platform, and regular password changes are some of the practices you can build into your habits.

## 11.5. Utilizing Privacy Settings on Social Media

Every reputable social media platform offers numerous controls for users to customize their privacy settings. Familiarize yourself with these tools and use them to your advantage. Set your profiles to private, customize who gets to see your posts, and limit the data you provide in your profiles.

## 11.6. Monitoring and Controlling Your Digital Footprint

Being mindful about your digital footprint can drastically improve your online security. Regularly review your privacy settings, be cautious about the amount and nature of personal data you share, and prune your existing digital footprint to reduce the risk of privacy violations.

## 11.7. Implementing Regular Social Media Clean-Up

Just as you regularly clean up your physical space, you should also periodically clean up your virtual one. This might mean deleting sensitive posts, removing older, non-relevant or potentially detrimental content, or even pruning your friend or follower lists from time to time.

## 11.8. Understanding and Utilizing Encryption

Encryption plays a significant role in safeguarding your online communication. Implement end-to-end encryption for your emails and messaging applications whenever possible, and understand the basics of public and private key encryption as it applies to your digital communications.

# 11.9. Being Conscious of Shared Networks and Devices

Lastly, being cautious about shared networks and devices is essential for secure online presence. Avoid logging in to your professional social media accounts using public computers or on unsecured wireless networks. If unavoidable, ensure to log out completely and clear any saved login details.

Final Thoughts

In conclusion, securing your online presence is not a one-off event, but a continuous process that requires you to be vigilant, proactive, and informed. It's a process of adapting your habits and behaviors to the ever-changing landscape of the digital world. It's about understanding the value of the data you have and taking appropriate steps to protect it. The effort is a small price to pay for maintaining and enhancing your professional image, potential opportunities, and for peace of mind in the Social Media Age. This security consciousness is necessary to avoid the devastating effects a compromised account can have on your professional reputation and career progression.